MW01595429

Beautiful and STRANGE

A Collection of Thoughts and Poetry

Jerica D. Wortham

Beautiful and Strange

Cover Art: M.Green

Dedication

This book is dedicated to anyone that *almost* thought they couldn't do it. Here's to blowing your own mind!

a piece of my heart

A letter to all that may cross this page
To those that may find themselves entangled in the
very essence of me
That will learn that my existence cannot be placed
inside of an intricately wrapped box
Those that waited for the arrival not knowing it
would be me
WELCOME
This is for those that stood by patiently as I made
the journey into myself
As I have come into my own
I have walked in shoes I never thought I could fill
Lived life in eras of sweetened tart
My life has been the sacrifice
I offer a piece of my heart
To those that wouldn't let me not believe
And when sadness came reminded me to His word
to cling
To those that couldn't care less about superficial
accolades
To girlfriends, and boyfriends
Barbecue and spades
To speechlessness
And words of thanks I know not how to start
My humbleness is present
I'm offering a piece of my heart
To those that kept it real
To those that kept it fake
To those whose soul I'm forever bound

4

To the Saturday morning bacon grease crackling
sound
To those that *really* know me
And love me anyway
To parents, and friends
To those that paved the way
To the spirit of deliverance as strong as a Red
River's part
I am here
I am grateful
I am the peace of my heart

genius

They call me genius because my selection of verbs,
nouns and adjectives flow just as naturally as the
Nile
Because they get this feeling of euphoria as they
reminisce about the time they felt like I feel
They call me genius not knowing this supposed
genius comes from them
I am but a mirror reflecting what I see
Showing them the poems that are inside of
themselves
How can I take credit what has been there all
along?
I only repeat what I hear
Attempt to make other see what I see
And yet they call me genius
Because of my supposed eloquence in speech
Because they hear three of my hundreds of poems
and assume the rest must be equally as great
They call me genius not knowing a genius wouldn't
have half the creative struggle as I do
They call me genius because they don't believe
they can do what I do
Not knowing they live what I write
Not knowing that my poetry is but a carbon copy of
their existence

Not knowing that my chorus serves no justice to
their verse
But they call me genius
G
E
N
I
U
S
Could you use that in a sentence?
I can give you two.
I am Jerica.
I am no genius.

what inspires me?

So what inspires me?
The wind
The way she floats from place to place to place
Able to touch everyone in some way
The way that even though some won't admit it, she
makes them feel alive
She can come as gently as a mother's touch
Or as fierce as a woman's score
She has a mission
She may rustle some leaves
She may make some waves
She gets there all the same
Not weighed down by the superficial substances of
the earth
Except for the times she carries those that couldn't
make it alone
So what inspires me?
The wind

what do you know?

I can't say I have moments of nostalgia, when I
reminisce about the first time
My mind
Conjured up the idea that being black wasn't a
good thing
I was eight and Benjamin told me he could never
be my boyfriend because I was of color
I can't pretend my eyes don't want to cry as I see
photos of strange fruits hanging from trees all
across the south
And when I hear tales of my people struggling to
keep their identity and having it stripped from
them
Tell me
What do you know about my tribal dancing
Ocean crossing
Cotton picking ancestors
Not a thing
Because "back then" it didn't matter
So now I'm left struggling to figure out where I
come from
Left to ponder about the family that was left
behind, and the life they have had to endure
Tell me
What do you know about my civil rights leading

We shall overcome singing
Open heart surgery performing
Traffic light inventing brothers and sisters?
Those that made significant impressions on the
world
And unknowingly set that tone for my burden
Don't get it twisted!
These people have done more than words can
express
Because of them my burden is deeper
My burden it's deeper than being pulled over for
what seems to be no reason at all
Deeper that hands up
Deeper than I can't breath
Deeper than saying another name
Deeper than having to give 200% in all things to be
considered equal....
Maybe...
It's harder than staying true to my heritage but still
managing to function in "outside" world
It's deeper and heavier because it not supposed to
be this way
I recall hearing stories of great men and women
dying so it could be different
And hearing of laws saying this wrong
So when I'm in the midst of all that supposed to be
eliminated only increases my burden

So I ask
What do you know about my
Bee boppin
Hip hoppin
Truth droppin people
I bet less than you think
Tell me
What do you know about my
Hard knocks living
Difference making
Burden bearin' people
Not much
But since the learning of his-story can cure the
repetition of it
You will soon learn more
My hope...
One day
All burdens will be dropped
All tears will be dried
And all thoughts of inferiority
Abolished

this would be great

I just wanna sit under a big ol' tree
Shoes off, breeze through my toes
Flower in my hair
Butterfly near my hand
Thinking about nothing

Who cares?

I've got this poem and it doesn't rhyme
It's not full of all those fancy words you learn in
English
It's just a series of letters
Places into words
And then formed into phrases
In hopes of changing someone's life for the better
I've got this poem
Without the slightest bit of rhythm
It's full of schisms and isms and things that make it
choppy
I've
Got
This
Poem
 Man
And this poem don't rhyme

It's not full of big words with complex meaning
But my poems got a voice
A voice so loud
A tone so rich
It can touch the soul of the heartless
Can bring hope to the hopeless
And give vision to the blind
I've got this poem
And it can't change the world
But it can change the way you think about your
brother
It can change the way you treat your sister
And make you reevaluate the way you feel about
the decisions you make
I've got this poem
And it don't rhyme
It has no rhythm
And won't be full of those terms you learned in
Creative Writing 101
But it's a poem
It's my poem
And I won't rest until it's heard

i don't like cats

I don't like cats
So when this white somebody with black spots
came up to me I thought about kicking it
But not sensing the threat he came up to me
Rubbed his body against me
Stood back, and jumped in my lap
He then rested his head against me
And MADE me pet him
I deliberated on throwing him across the porch
Then I remembered
Sometimes you just need to be held
So I sat there with this old dirty cat that probably
hasn't been held in a long time
And watch the grass grow

performance piece

I use to write performance pieces
A series of fictitious situations
Filled with clever one liners
That made the audience roar with excitement

I wrote performance pieces
They reflected none of me
Had none of my image intertwined but that's what
they wanted
So I wrote them
Performed them
They loved them
They came back for more

Until the day I realized I was afraid to do me, afraid
to display the true poem inside
I had become an expert at performing lies
So now we shall try this performance piece on for
size

I was born in Tulsa, OK
The second of what I thought my mother's three
My favorite color is yellow
It's a reflection of me

I sing often
Probably more than my daddy likes
When I was 7 years old someone stole my bike

I have 3 fathers, and to say it best
I think my life represents Gods ultimate patience
test
I've been in love 2 times and one of them doesn't
know it
The feelings went deep but I was afraid to show it

I was never a bad child
But I know the meaning of misfit
Never hung with a clique because they would
never get
Me
I trust no one totally
I love to smile and I do it joyfully

I have many associates
Only a FEW real friends
World's greatest listener and on advice....
Well...
It depends

I'm a Gemini
Gods teaching me it means nothing
I have a loving Pastor that wants me to be
something
Most of the men in my life love their either brown
or white
I pray and I pray
But may never win the fight
It's their battle and I wish I had a saddle

16

'Cause I haven't ridden a horse since I was three

Look at me!
On stage performing for my mama
And daddies
Grandma Mary too
For Daddy McGee
And Ms. Clayton
For Lansing
And Lovie
KJ
And Siani
For anybody that knows anybody connected to
these bodies
To all the hugs I wished I had
The I love you(s) I was afraid to accept
To all the truth that is coming
Thank you
I love the Lord
He heard my cry
I've crossed that river a thousand times
To bring you this
My performance piece
My life manifested to paper and ink
Mixed with a series of factual situations
No clever one liners to make you roar with
excitement
But I wrote it
Performed it, Loved it
And if you want no more
I understand

brand New

Brand new
So I call it my hot fiyah
Number one scorching
Thirst quench supplier
Grade A resume
And new hire
Putting in so much work after this I may retire
This is that new spit
That "get on the mic" and just rock spit
That spent too long at the bottom so it's my get on
top spit
My yea I may get on stage and flop spit
But I'm giving it my all because it's my told I ain't
gonna be ish spit
Foul mouth, been bluffin
Emancipation's calling me out
But I find walks of faith leave little room for false
doubt
Wide hips
Accenting full lips
Nappy roots like buckwheat
Soul food's keeping me thick
Transformed
Flesh versus spirit's keeping me torn
I die to myself daily because I am labeled reborn
And yo I love words
Nouns, adjectives and adverbs

I know it sounds crazy but *I'ma* try my hand at
Proverbs
31:10
Knowing true happiness comes from within
If integrity is your character you no longer have to
pretend
I'm perfectly
IMPURFEKT
Get on the mic and murk it
Found myself growing and who knew that it would
hurt a bit
Old ties
Drowned by burgers and hot fries
I was sad when them size sevens could no longer
hold my thighs
Don't get it twisted
I'm still hot like blocks on Front Street
Grandma's peach cobbler is still so sweet
I remember mama working three jobs to keep
shoes on my feet
He says I'm bitter when I don't smile
Peace of mind now on trial
Dead woman walking I say this could be my green
mile
And some say she's so strange
Got crazy flow 'cause she deranged
Only shot of freedom is if she pleads insane
When I just want to be
In laymen's terms be free
Living inside a box just aint my cup of tea
Insomniac

Yes it seems I'll never tire
Got flooded with life now I search for ground that's
higher
When I reached the top was crowned neo-soul
survivor
Take heed and listen cause these words I speak are
dire
Giving them to you for free
So for the demand I'm top supplier
Expressions come at no cost but I'll sale to the
highest buyer
Brand new

no subject

No subject
Just paper and ink
The words manifestations of exactly what I think
So you say
I am infatuated
Is that the truth?
If it ain't then don't fake it
Are you happy?
Whenever you see me
Elated?
If I tell you what I am thinking
This could be the end
My clairvoyance is beginning to begin
All over
I see images so clear
When you get closer
I'm left wishing you were near
When you leave
Tears start to come
I could clear them all up
With a liter of coke and some rum
Yum
Yum
Yum
Sop it up with a biscuit I won't leave a crumb

Thought you knew
The earth doesn't stop
The tick of the clock
The tock of the clock
I am amazed
When you pass my way
I hear you when you speak
But you have nothing to say
To me
It's just a bunch of jazz
'Cause nothing from nothing leaves
You do the math
I'm out!

who knew?

Behind the eyes
Darkness
Behind the eyes
Pain
Behind the eyes
Mirrors of tomorrow
Shattered by yesterday
Behind the eyes
Thought
Behind the eyes
Change
Behind the eyes
A unique piece of mind
Hidden from all range

dependability

What happened to dependability?
You know
The time when people did what they said they
would do
When someone's word was as strong as Earth's
gravitational pull
And the thought of "what if they don't fall
through?" never entered your mind
Good old dependability
Who has it these days?
Who has the ability to be where they say they will
be when they say they will be there
To go where they say they will go when they say
they will go there
To do what they say they will do when they say
they will do it
Can I get someone I can count on?
Even buses have five minute windows
In times like this
And situations as this
They wonder why I depend on no one but myself

stolen rights
(For my friend that couldn't find the words)

I said no
He said yes
It hurt
He kept going
I wanted to die
But he kept going
And while I cry
The thought keeps going through my head
I said no
He said yes
My physical strength no match for his
I fought
He kept going
I cussed but he kept going
Alone in my room the thought keeps going
Through my head
No one knows
Not even my closest friends
I am embarrassed and don't want eyes to look my
way
Can't go public
Mama would cry too hard
Daddy would question his ability to protect
And other would question the validity

I said no
He said yes
I had the right
And he took it

proprietor

I am the owner of pain
I didn't buy it
It was given to me
This morning I woke up to the sound of the phone
ringing
The person on the other end said he had more than
he could keep for himself
So he shared it with me
Or maybe I with him
So now together we own pain
We are its caregivers
We have given it a place to reside
I don't know how long it will stay
But being its owner I am forced to keep it until
someone takes it
Or breaks it's
Cycle
I am the owner
By inheritance
I receive this prize by default

DNA

Through my veins flows the only part of you not
able to be tarnished by reality
Through each artery and ventricle is a piece of you
keeping me alive
Giving me just enough strength to keep going
No matter what life dealt to me
Or what our relationship may have been
It's still you running through me
It you that has placed an imprint so deep on my
mind even the *unthought* thoughts get stuck inside
Then I in them
Like you in me
Running through my veins
Keeping my heart
Although broken
Strong
Strong enough to forgive and love

The Home Going

(I remember coming home and writing everything down... I *needed* to remember verbatim)

Monday morning rush
Me and A.P. running late again
We're to meet at 9:30 and it's already 10
And we must go to the store to get some last
minute things
Knowing as soon as we get to Bigma's there's going
to be a scene
We finally make it
And there isn't much of a fuss
We just dress and sit
And wait for the limo to come for us
A.P. is really stressed
You can see it in her face
Thing haven't gone right for her
Yet she handles it with grace
We step into the limo and we're all ready to part
While the reality of this moment begins to plague
my heart
We make it to the church, but I am feeling weak
We line up two by two on the side of the street
Bigma and "Daddy"
Then me and A.P.

The others in no particular order at least as I could
see
From the stairs to the entrance
From the entrance to the sanctuary
Everyone there had a look of pity and despair
Me and A.P. hold hands all the way to the chair
There we are smack dab in front of the coffin
Just the thought of him being inside made the tears
start to droppin'
I did not say a word I just held my sister close
A lady began to sing
Some began to boast
On how good God was
The song was "I won't complain"
I just remember "hallelujah anyway"
The service is soon over after my uncle's words are
said
Then like militant little ants they line up to see Big
Red
Each one passing with a hug, a hand, or kiss
The words were very much appreciated
But I certainly will not miss
Hearing
"Be strong"
"I'm so sorry for your loss"
"If you need anything let me know"
The congregation was gone

Or shall I say the congregation had left
It was now our turn to view the honorary guest
I swear I wanted to be strong
I wanted not to cry
But the tears they kept filling up my sorrow ridden
eyes
While I help his cold hard hands
The tears fell on his face
The face I didn't kiss until it was too late
I remember thinking
His eyes are just like mine
His eyebrows I straightened so every hair would be
in line
His face was swollen
They said fluid was trapped in there
But mostly he looked peaceful so about that I did
not care
He had on a money green suit
The one hand that showed it held the bible
The other one was tucked away because his bullet
ridden hand was not as pliable
Now it's time to leave
Once again two by two
Leaving thought the very entrance in which we can
through
Me and A.P. walk down the stairs in perfect sync
Left and right

Our feet creating a beat
For the blues that are playing in our hearts
Waiting for all the family members to get in the car
I sit and wonder will this trip be very far
Everyone's talking and laughing
I just sit and look out onto the street
They're reminiscing on old times
I have no memories on which to speak
We make it to the gravesite
Where there are more in this sorrowful basket
One of them bereaving a little pink casket
And they say she only lived on day
Well hallelujah, hallelujah, hallelujah anyway
We sit and we pray
Me and A.P. crack some jokes
A large spider crawling on me
A.P. wipes away with one smooth stroke of the
hand
And with a few flowers from Dad's casket I head to
the caravan
Where again I ride in silence
Hating to hear those faithful words
"Are you ok?"
Because I'm tired of lying and saying "yes"
But the worst part is over
Now we're getting to the best

The church family prepared dinner for the family
and guests
Some of it good
Some of it not
But most importantly all of it hot
A spray reading "Dad" is in plain view
It's now hard to swallow but I make it through
Hallelujah anyhow
Hallelujah anyway
God is still good!
As Bigma would say

It hurts when I remember, even more when I forget

I thought about you today
I almost picked up the phone to call
And then I remembered
 You weren't here anymore
I didn't cry
Just took a deep breath and sighed
I didn't cry
I just took a nap
I thought of you today
What type of things you would be up to
Was the sun I felt just as warm on your back
And then I remembered
You weren't here anymore
I didn't cry
Just took a deep *deep* breath and sighed
I didn't cry
I just swallowed as hard as I could
I thought of you today
In the middle of class
 While my professor reviewed litigation
I saw your face
That face
The one I didn't kiss until it was too late
And I laughed

Thinking of how much A.P. looks like you
How when she's angry her eyebrow move close
together like yours do
And then I remembered
You weren't here anymore
I didn't cry
I just took a deep *deep deep* breath and sighed
I didn't cry
I just decided to get it right next time

"Daddy"
(I still remember the smile on your face when I
read this to you)

Weak, feeble hands not able to grasp as they once
did
Eyes that see not as well
A body moving not as fast getting him where he
needs to go
A façade of being just as able as always
With a mouth just as quick as before
My grandfather sits before me

"No doctor can tell me $#!+" he would exclaim as
he took his religious dose of Vitamin C and Garlic
Followed by his 'tassium' hidden cleverly in his
daily banana
Stories of him and his pieces of women scattered
strategically across the United States
Photo albums filled with laughter long before my
time
Tears long before my time
Filled with the remnants of a struggle long before
my time
My grandfather stands before me

The infectious sounds of them "down home blues"
can be heard from his long deserved red Cadillac
Witnesses of his rhythmic shuffled across laughter
filled rooms
Traces of the scent of hay left un-regretfully in his
shirts and pants
A raggedy mutt named Apollo constantly being
scolded
Clearly displaying the upper hand
With tattered shoes not as shiny
And shoe laces not as durable
My grandfather dances before me
Singing a song
Singing his song
That prayerfully I'll one day understand

"Daddy Homegoing"
(I wonder what you would have thought of this)

I won't say it doesn't hurt
Or that I still don't cry
Won't say I'm not angry that you can't pick up the
line
When I call
Or that my heart does not hunger or thirst
For just one more time for us to converse
But I know that my tears cannot measure the
worth
Of a man as a man
And the legacy of his birth

You gave me a father
And a sister
Auntie, uncles, and cousins galore
Real life lessons and so much more
So for what it's worth
Here's to you Big Blue
'Cause I want you to know I'm remembering you
Pepper colored grey hair
Wire framed lenses
Your meticulous way of staying in my business
Hay scented shirts
With a red Cadillac to match

Faded jeans
And trucker hats
Being a man
A man's man
But still giving your dog Apollo the upper hand
Random *YeeHaws* for no apparent reason
Road trips to Denver during summer seasons
Being Daddy
Which was more than enough
Moving me into the dorms using a flatbed truck
Beating me, Ariel, and JaRee's behind
When we walked the track to the next counties line
For saying I "better make that fat boy a good wife"
And telling me that I can't rush through life
And so you know your labor wasn't in vain
And that my heart will still melt at the sound of
your name
And that I offer thanks for you always being
authentically you
I'll stand here and say
I'm remembering you
In every sunset over railroad tracks
In every fishing line that gets caught when flung
back
In every spring break
In every pasture
In every smile at the thought of your laughter

In salads without dressing
And wild onion in bloom
In you not allowing me to grow up to soon
In memories of you always having a hand to lend
In memories of you as a grandpa and friend
In wedding day dances
In big strong hands
In every cow, horse, goose, pig, or raccoon I'll ever
encounter in this land
In B.B.King
In Bobby Blue Bland
In every time I hear Muddy Waters sing "aint that a
man"
In every time I look into an uncle's eyes
In every time I refuse to give up and not try
In every time I thank Jesus, or put God first
I am remembering and honoring the worth
Of a man as a man
And the legacy of his birth

So Daddy I won't say it doesn't hurt
Or that I still don't cry
Or that I'm not angry you can't pick up the line
When I call
Or that my heart does not hunger or thirst
For just one more time for us to converse

But I know that my tears cannot measure the
worth
And I know that my fears cannot measure the
worth
And I know that my years cannot measure the
worth
Of a man as a man
And the legacy of his birth

part scratch braid (3/6/11)

(Again... I felt overwhelmingly compelled to
document this moment....5 days later you were
gone)

Part
Scratch
Braid

Part
Scratch
Braid

I'm not tender headed she said
I tried hard to believe her

Part
Scratch
Braid

"Thank you Jesus" she would whisper

Part
Scratch
Braid

She said, "They sent me home to die"

I begged her to fight
She said she would
I tried hard to believe her

Part
Scratch
Braid

Half the form she once was

Part
Scratch
Braid

Yet stronger than ever

Part
Scratch
Braid

Ebony defeat her stature
Ivory hope her eyes

Part
Scratch
Braid

She said she doesn't know how God's gonna fix this
But she's living to be a testimony

Part
Scratch
Braid

I stand over her in silence
Not wanting to sound unwise

Part
Scratch
Braid

Not wanting to show how angry I am at God
Or the doctor, or nurses

Part
Scratch
Braid

Tears in her eyes she thank me
I try hard to believe her
I have done NOTHING

Part
Scratch

Braid

She is still before me plagued with the same
diagnosis
I feel helpless

Part
Scratch
Braid

Ashamed of taking my own life for granted

Part
Scratch
Braid

Ashamed of thinking of my own life when hers
hangs in the balance

All I could do
All I could do
Was...

Part
Scratch
Braid

Part
A prayer in every part that just as God parted the
red sea and delivered his children from bondage
He would deliver her from this bondage

Scratch
And scratch
And scratch
Hoping to somehow soothe an ailing spirit
Encourage a heart needing to know it'd be ok

Braid
Strand over strand
Strand over strand
A *rythmatic* chant of victory

Strand over strand
For the Father

Strand over strand
For the Son

Strand over strand
For the Holy Spirit

Forming one braid

46

One faith
One hope
Many times over

She said, "they sent me home to die"
I *begged* her to fight
She said she would
I tried *haaaaaaard* to believe her….

Part
Scratch
Braid

I believe her.

healing

I change her dressing
Expose tribal markings
War scars
Victory banner
All in one
Eyes do rain dances
Beckon praise
Never been so happy to hurt so much
We are thankful
Lips haven't touched cigarette butts in weeks
Food tastes sweeter
Healing isn't always pretty
Healing is a road
A long winding road
And it keeps you up while you travel
Twists faces like
Soda pop tops
We are healing
It ain't pretty
But my God, it is beautiful

my apologies

My apologies to the young black brother on the 222 this
evening
Clothes dingy
Hands permanently stained by motor oil, and other
mechanical devices
Trying to find his way to the nearest family dollar
Me watching suspiciously as the bus stops then goes
again
Knowing the answer to the questions he's posed but my
mouth refusing to answer
My lips just won't move
All I could do was watch as he gazes out into the street
Praying for the welcoming sight of the fluorescent red
sign
All I could think is that it's only a few blocks up the road
If you could just hold on for a few more moments, I
could point you in the right direction
Just as soon as my lips can separate and keep you from
having to face these brutal winds
But all I could do was watch as he requested for the bus
to stop
All I could think was NO! Not yet!
It's not your time
As I watched you to face the cold winter evening alone
Because I was too afraid to tell you this bus would be
turning soon and taking you exactly where you need to
go
So, I just sat back

Closed my eyes
And allowed the steady motion of the bus to massage
away the guilt
My apologies to the young, black brother on the 222
Just trying to make his way
I was afraid to tell you then
But your destination is not too far away
Just sit back
Hold on, be patient
And allow this vessel to lead you there

to my brothers caught in the struggle

I don't quite know the feeling of forming a dream
Grasping a dream
Losing a dream
Obtaining a dream
Then learning that that dream came with more than it
originally presented feels like
But I know what it feels like when I see your step a little
less carefree
When I see that face where happiness once dwelled
replaced with despair
And speech filled with an undertone of sorrow
I don't know what it feels like to want to be and not to
be
Or to dedicate countless hours to a struggle I could only
hope to overcome
To know the end is coming but realizing it can't come
too soon
I don't know the feeling
But I know what it feels like when I see your heart
breaking
And when I see you wanting to give more but not
having it in you
I don't know how it feels when you see frustration on
my face and not know how to relieve it
When you must explain to me again that you don't have
what it takes
To my brothers in the struggle
Keep your head up

in the dark

Who's afraid of the dark?
"Not I" said the lion
"Not I" said the bear
"Not I" said the colored girl with long kinky hair
Who's afraid to change the world?
"Maybe the bear" said the lion
"Maybe the lion" said the bear
"Maybe me" said the colored girl with long kinky hair

the best time ever

When no one is watching
I am free
 I am only who I know how to be
There's no need to be heard
No need to use words
When no one's watching
Silence is everything but still
Thoughts manifesting to creations so real
When no one is watching
I close my eyes
Think of heaven
Pray to be wise
When no one is watching
I am, who I am
Nothing more, nothing less
I am the control in the center of mess
When no one is watching
And I am all alone
I sing in my heart "Sunday kind of love" songs
Knowing I don't need what I claim I do
Knowing whatever I feel now is true
When no one is watching, I can only see
The type of person I strive to be

beautiful

If no one's ever told you
I'm telling you
You are beautiful
Not only because of you
But because of the legacy within you
You are the sons and daughters of those that made
ways out of none
Provided hope without funds
And made you unique
If no one's ever told you
I am telling you
You are beautiful
Kinda like the sound of "Yesterday"
As the great Miles Davis begins to play
You are beautiful because of your own eclectic style of
walk, talk, and dance
You are the song and the rhythm of this land
So, if no one's ever told you
I'm telling you
You are beautiful
Although magazines done seem to favor your tone
Or fashion give thought to the voluptuousness of your
bones
I know it's hard to find your beauty when your hair is
not as straight as others
When no class has class enough to teach you about
your brothers
And sisters

If no one's ever told you
I'm telling you
You are beautiful
Even when the media creates a tapestry of disgrace
At least in reference to your race
Leaving you to fill in the gaps
Forcing you to keep will enough to force other to see
you for who you are
I understand it can be hard to see your beauty when
your mouth don't talk the way they say it should talk
When your hair doesn't fall the way, they say it should
fall
And your face has the trace of melancholy and
frustration
So, in case no one has told you
I'm telling you
You are beautiful
Not only for who you are
But for the legacy that is in you
You are beautiful because there is no other way that
you could be
You are the fresh fruits of our nation's family tree
Says our forefathers
And their fathers too
So, take hold of your beauty
And let your beauty shine through

things fall apart

Things fall apart
Like Shakespearean and Greek tragedies, we all play our
part
Even if it's the chorus
Come on let's explore this
Stripped from the mother land now tell me what the
score is
Well so far, the U.S. is up forty acres and a mule
Plus, the exploitation of black athletes in school
They laughed when I was a slave
Now they laugh that I'm free
Cause Willie Lynch taught them to build the prisons in
me
Now I'm too hard to be a lady
And he's too soft to be a man
And we teach our children that success doesn't belong
in our hands
I don't know about you
But I'm the lineage of a survivor
I sniff history every morning those facts they leave me
higher
Even when I get frantic
Reminiscing brothers and sister at the bottom of the
Atlantic
Stay holding it together
Praying for good
But so use too bad whether
Astonished by life even after X and Ms. Parks

Then sadly I remember that some things just fall apart.

growing

Why does growing hurt so much?
Perhaps it's the stretching of ideas
Maybe the detachment of the eyes
Allowing them to roam and explore the unfamiliar
Could it be the breaking of hearts that come through
giving of emotion often kept under wraps?
It's the change
So why does growing hurt so much?
It's the breaking of the skin
The shedding of old ways
Being covered by the cold and un-intimate touch of
conviction
Why does growing hurt so much?
Because the blue jeans of deception and the t-shirts of
self-righteousness no longer fit
The waist cuts
The t shirt overshadows
And you ask why growing hurts so much
Its change
Status quo is no longer accepted

Consistory

My life is the consistory
Of intellectually
Analytical
Enigmas dressed as mysteries
A city of sweet
In a state called misery
Remnants of sugar cane mixed with history
I'm taking steps until they turn into miles
Tilling the ground until I turn into Miles
Davis
And reflect on yesterday
My mind and lips never missing a chance to replay
Or relay some truth
Impregnate you with hope
My plan to get you higher than that fire
Side effects longer than trench coats
But to tell you the truth
I get tired of complacent figures
 More concerned with rims
And Timbs
And how to stack their figures
Than how they can help their brother man
Yet the words I spit seem to only get buried in the sands
of time
Lost in the rhyme
I guess they're tired of trying
But then again, who am I to judge
And through the spirit of redemption

Who am I to hold the grudge
Nobody's perfect
We just be who we be
Yet they are looking and listening
And still can't see or hear me
Touching
But still can't feel me
Cause the things that once seemed obsolete
Occupy more of my life than I could ever believe
I pray and receive
A light from above
'cause now the push for success feels more like a shove
And I can't help but get tripped up
As I slip up
And get placed in a position where I'm forced to face up
to the fact that
Nothing's what it seems
Life is but a dream
And I am forced to cling to this world that is sinfully
sublime
Holding on to a dream I thought could never be mine
Like the time
I loved him
Trust it was no façade
But happiness is not an option when you try to turn a
man into God
But my love life now is better than I ever thought it
could be
And like Whitney the love I went searching for was
found inside of me

And like Paul
I know what it's like to have plenty
Then again, I know what it's like to lack
But I am thankful I serve a God that's able to pick up the
slacks
And though His love seems to defy all logic
His spirit to me is nothing short of cathartic
And if you don't know it
You could be labeled lethargic
Or
Asleep
But the ideas of what those repercussions could bring
Could make the strongest man weep
And now and days I find my mouth too weak to speak
But who needs words
When actions say enough
When hands get, roughed and callused when sisters are
hard at work
And multiple roles have us constantly changing shirts
Or was that hats?
My friend Chris would be like "Yo, that's enough of
that"
Enough crying
Enough dying
But never will it be enough trying
'cause I refuse to give up on my peeps
No matter what their hustling
And bustling
And shiftlessness may reap
I love them as much as I love myself

Their place in my life is like a book on a shelf
It just makes sense
So, as I continue on my stream of steady increasing
motivation
And some continue on their streams of steady
increasing self-deprivation
So, deeper I find my words in sands of time
Lost inside of rhymes
I guess they're tired of trying
So, in frustration they get tired and move away
Hey
There's a lot to be said when there's nothing more to
say
When there's nothing more to say, I hear its best to
keep your mouth shut
'cause your next few words
Could spark
A revolution

shining

I ride through existence on air
Reaching all within my grasp
Seldom touching
Yet felt all the same
Bringing change
For the will of will
And the wheels for will
For I am the will
And I mourn
With this overwhelming guilt
As for a moment, I actually thought I was the way
Yet it turns out I was only in the way
Of
The Way
Yet I shine
Like the reflection in sunlight
I shine
Like "that girl", Stevie sings vividly in song
I shine
Using my love to make men strong
So, I guess that makes me in sense a spinal cord
That connects to the neck
Bringing a system of support and keeping the head up
Riiiiiiight
 On
And on and on and on
My cypher keeps moving like a rolling stone
Like Badu

Hachooo
Bless you
And you
And you
And me should just sit and reflect some time
Buy and sale some time
So, we can make some time
For the future
Is knocking on the door
And I am just dying to let it in
'Cause success is next of kin to me
I mean my family tree
Is filled with the fruits of labors as far as the eye can see
So, far Ms. Jerica don't think she's going blind
So, while I'm soaring through existence
Using the force of my determination to keep me afloat
As I carry the sun in the palm of my hands and cast
shadows of myself on all creation
I get this feeling
And I can't as of now name its location
But it's a mixture of butterflies
And that feeling you get when your body gets lethargic
And everything is everything
And nothing else matters except that I am riding on air
On faith
And I'm too afraid to look down
I'm too afraid to look up
I'm too afraid to look forward
 I'm too afraid to look back
So, all I have to look at is myself

And I make choices for betterment
I make choices for *upliftment* of you and me
Because although we are all different we are part of the same
Family tree
Of life
So, I decide to move forward
Even though my arms are getting tired
And the wind is cutting my face
And the sun is getting hot on these finger tips
I move forward
Even though my friends may say I'm being over zealous
I move forward
Because maybe all they need is a path
Some light shed
And since I pride myself in having a little light in me
I move forward
And I *shiiiiiine* through this existence that I am in
And I invite you
To shine with me

no apologies

Apologize for what?
Being young, gifted, and black
Young, fly, and saved
And able to switch hats
At the drop of a hat from this gig to that
Switch flows like styles
Switch styles like racks
Grieve?
Boo!
Never!
I was born this way
And I'll keep saying words that make people say
I've got to do better
Next stop's the top
Donny Hathaway
A path away
Through this cream of the crop
'Cause I hated being quiet when I knew I should've
spoke
And I hated speaking up when I wished that I could
choke
On words
That brought tears to your eyes
But those words made you better so I won't apologize
I can't say that I'm sorry for bridges burned
For mistakes made for they are lessons learned
For being smart
Or beautiful

Or incredibly stacked
There's enough sorry folks in the world
I'll let them handle that

open mic

I woke up needing it
Like air to lungs oxygen consuming breathing it
Life
Condensed into capsule sized form
Swallowing it
It's necessary!
Absolutely necessary!!!
I pour it out of my mouth the end result could be
legendary
Sometime I think I am less than what I need to be
Heart beat sustained existence it bleeds thru me
Like this pen
It don't write like it use to
It scratches on paper but the truth it cannot come to
It's too real when you write it
Easier to ignore it then to fight it
Gasoline tears, etched stains, begging to be ignited
To feel something!
It's primal
By instinct I am drawn
To this place
This stage
This altar
This sanctuary
It's complicated
This desire to connect
Soul to soul
Breast to breast

I speak

Afraid

Because speaking only leaves room for error.

And silence

Silence is now my only friend.

When I've got a million things to say but no words...

But I guess

I guess

I've gotten use to the quiet...

I guess

I guess

I guess I'll go outer space

Jupiter maybe... No mercury!

Yeah that's where I'll go

It could get cold better grab a jacket

I need this!

Like walls need graffiti

Yea I need this

Like deprivation needs the needy

Disappointed

because tears fall on mercury too

I found that out the hard way

No escape

So, I start thinking about silly shit!

Mercury

You know There's a lot of interesting facts about

mercury

It's a small planet

Closets to the sun

Which by the nature of its homonym makes me think of the son
So maybe I'm right where I need to be
And true to the mercurial nature it comes over me
Like hot lava it's bubbles up inside me
I am ticking
A Tic-king time bomb is what I am. Ready to explode on the next muthafucka that thinks they want it. Tired of placing nice...
Nice is what I was when I kept quiet
Nice is what I was when I traded my dignity in place of your life...
So, I said fuck it!
I'll write it all
I'll write it *alllll*
I mean I need this right
Mmmm I need this
I need this like
The river needs the rain
I need this
Like masochists need pain
So, I went there
Mined deep in search of those elements
Precious in nature
Products of pressure
Pretty sure
I need this
At the corner of crazy and insane Milli has the paintbrush I just have a pen and I said I'll write it. I'll write it all... Tell the story they said ... Tell it all!

So I wrote it!
Everything!
Everything!!!
Every muthafuckin line
And I signed it!
Signed sealed delivered I'm yours
I'm yours
On the corner
the corner of crazy and insane
I wrote it all!!
Everything!
Every inch of time
Every word I said engraved in your mind
Arrested, tried, and sentenced to unspoken crimes
Truths written, twisted, tangled, in the tapestry of
rhyme
I live I love I speak JParle' was the fine
And I left it there!

courteous

No need to run when I hold the door open for you
No need to rush
No need to think my kindness will soon run out
This is my love offering to you
So don't take what I am using to make your life easier as
an inconvenience
Don't run
Take your time
The doorway will be here

going

Going, going, going
Going, going, gone
Moving moving, moving
Moving, moving, moving, on
Staying, staying, staying,
Staying staying, staying strong,
On my way, on my way,
On my way, home

love jones

So I'm loungin'
And then he walks in
A suave lookin' brotha with mad dividends
He says, " Hey girl let me holla a sec"
As I examine his biceps and the curve of his pecks
He says " Suga why don't you give me your hand
We could travel to Rome, Egypt, Asia, and France"
I said, " Man Boo that all sounds swell"
As he gives play by play of him ringing my bell
My head is spinning
An enigma I'm in
As he explains I can have caddy, hummer, and Benz
But something's not right
I mean it's all too much
I was just chillin' in the Cafe trying to eat me some lunch
He says," My queen I could give you ice and chrome"
I said, "That's the bomb babe but I'm savin' myself for
the
Jones
The Love Jones, the Jones of Jones'
Jones has mocha colored skin and a wonderful smile
He makes the world I'm livin' in seem all worthwhile
He makes me laugh
I never cry
He explores my soul through the gaze of his eyes
I mean I'm iggin
'cause technically he's not mine,
But I can tell by his actions that he is worth the time

To get to know
Over and over
My heart keeps dancing in this field of clovers
He the shhhhhhh
So Mr. debonair don't take this the wrong way
It's just my frame of mind seems always stay
On this jones
This Loves Jones
The jones of Jones'
I mean.....
Perhaps you could impress the other girls
With the promises of everything
in a material world
But I'm lookin' for somethin'
more than just a little bit real
I'm lookin' for something my
great great grandma could feel
You know that Jones
That Love Jones
That Jones of Jones'
I wish you could see when he
walks into a place
The ultra beams of light that reflect
off my face
He is my sunshine
And though he may be your rain
I'm savin' myself all the same
For the Jones, the Love Jones
The Jones of JONES

the search is over

You say you like them cool, calm, and collected
Nice humble and reflective
A man loves a woman who can respect him
So baby.... here I am

You like them confident but not arrogant
Realness wrapped in elegance
And in absence you'd crave her presence
Well brother...... here I am

You like them intelligent and classy
In speech not harsh or brassy
Never ever considered trashy
If you're lookin' than here I am

You like them submissive but no pushover
Can roll the pinto OR the rover
 Make your heart dance in fields of clover
 If that true than here I am

You want her to love you just for you
Not for what you've become in a month or two
Knowing whatever she speaks is true
No sense in frontin'
Here I am

You've made requests
They've been supplied

What's obvious can't be denied
I can run but cannot hide
If you're looking for a lady
Here I am….

personification

I dreamt of Love last night
Wrapped in flesh before my face
Every intricate detail in its rightful place
And it touched me
With its hand of admiration
With its fingers of elation
With its caress of adoration
And I smiled
I dreamt of Love last night
He kissed me on my cheek
My world no longer bleak
 I am happy
 From the thought of being wanted
When everything is fronted
I don't have to guess
And I smiled
I dreamt of love last night
And I prayed it not just that
I just want it back
But the alarm is going off

reincarnation

I loved you before I met you
Because I met you in my dreams
And I've been kissing you there so long it feels like
second nature
When we touch
And share ourselves
Amongst ourselves
Do you remember laughing in the corners of my mind?
Do you remember lying in my arms?
Where you rested your head so comfortably I could
barely stand it
Because I did it before I met you
In my dreams, I loved you
So now loving you is the only thing I know

r.e.m.

I'm at a dance
Hair combed
Look fly
See a man
Pants creased
Grabs his piece
I'm thinkin' man!
I'm kinda shy
Wonder why
He's in this pace
My attraction I can't erase
Should I be real?
Ask his name
Get his math
Say what's the deal
Sit him down
Have a drink
Say how I feel
He's looking tight
I'm feelin' right
I'd let him kill
I'll allow me one cheap thrill
So here we are
Face to face
Up in this place
My mouths ajar
Spittin' game
Never lame

I'm getting far
Hold up please
Gets on his knees
And raise the bar
Feelin rushed
But not Limbaugh
Man
He's got this rig
Or better rock
Knock off your socks
It makes me sing
This can't be right
Not what it seems
Ah man!
A dream!

bad reception

I've heard those words a hundred times
But my heart won't let it be real
And due to my own skepticism
I've devalued what you feel
I understand how frustrating to have your words taken
lightly
But I don't want to wait up to your definite being a
might be
See life for me ain't been no crystal stair
Still my cross I make you bare
It's not your fault
You just got caught
And I'm refusing to let go
Do I want to live without you?
The answer is no
It's almost sweet
And I almost beat
The system
 Of distrust
It's a must to trust somebody sometime
Why not let this time be my time?
Said he
Who me
Nah brother
Cause I've heard those words a hundred times
But my heart won't let me feel
So now you're left with the difficult task of convincing
me that it's real

lovin'

He gives me lovin'
One in a million lovin'
More than a man lovin'
Tell all my friends lovin'
He gives good lovin'
Melt my heart lovin'
Sending chills lovin'
1000 thrills lovin'
He gives addictive lovin'
Come back for more lovin'
Make me a fool lovin'
Got all the right tools lovin'
I got some lovin'
Sweet dreamin' lovin'
Holla, screamin', lovin'
Got me fiendin' lovin'
I got right lovin'
Pure in heart lovin'
Take me to church lovin'
Will sit and pray lovin'
I got his lovin'
Everyone's jockin' lovin'
This can't be true lovin'
All of mine lovin'
I got secluded lovin'
The only one lovin'
Brags about me lovin'
No hoes allowed lovin'

He gives delusional lovin'
Head over heels lovin'
Head in the clouds lovin'
Makin' me proud lovin'
He gives sweet lovin'
Diabetic lovin'
My heart is tamed lovin'
Never the same lovin'
He gives plentiful lovin'
Fill me up lovin'
Satisfied lovin'
Covered in sweat lovin'
He gives ambitious lovin'
Knows all my dreams lovin'
All my schemes lovin'
Never judgmental lovin'
He gives unconditional lovin'
Will you be my bride lovin'
Till death do us part lovin'
I promise I do lovin'
A house and kids lovin'
A cat and dog lovin'
I'm thankin' the Lord lovin'
Speakin' in tongues lovin

surreal

He keeps dancing a seafoam green in the crevices of my
mind
Metaphors leave his lips and a *surreality* creeps from
behind
Yellow colored skies
And fuchsia colored seas
Black mountains and pink plains
And like the rubber band on my wrist he keeps
stretching
And stretching
Never breaking
Because breaking is not an option
Failure is not an option
Because the myriad of heterochromatic he provides
wouldn't validate that
Or maybe it's just my imagination that would find it
absurd
But that step he does is right on time
In my mind
Full of yellow colored skies and fuchsia colored seas
Black mountain and pink plains
And like the rubber band on my wrist he keeps
stretching
And stretching
Never breaking
Because breaking is not an option.

no words

There aren't words for heartbeats skipped
Tossed like pebbles on ponds
Stomachs fluttered
Heads clouded
Hands hungry
Fed by skin
Sun kissed
Sun touched
Loved
There are no words for lips pressed
Souls shaken
Goose bumped arms
Knowing
Just knowing that you know that you know
I'm yours
And you're mine
And the world doesn't matter
This here is the matter
This moment
When I'm lying next to you
Breathing
Earplugs in
Snores tip toeing across pillows
Whispering to me that someone is near
That someone on this earth has the ability to tap into
me so deep I can hardly stand it
So deep it hurts
But in a good way

Like first times
Or massages
No words for I love you deep like
Deep like
Like….
No words….
So, silence becomes my friend
Because it's the only one that gets us
That gets this love that I haven't been able to describe
This love that penetrates the core
That's visible to the masses
The love that can't be immolated or duplicated
Patty caked
This is no child's play
No joke
Forever's no joke
 And you're the only one forever seems right with
No fear in love
Just existence
Just Mrs.
Wortham
To him
To me it's a badge of honor
To him
I wear it like he wears my long days on his mind
With the same passion and delicacy, he holds my heart
With the same concern, he views my destiny
With the same love, he pours into me each day
In a terrible way, he's the best thing that ever
happened to me

So, I love him *on purpose*
Making sure not to miss a spot
Not a drop of care left to chance
Living romance
Exhausting possibilities
Pissing people off with this greatness
I can't tell them about it anymore
They don't get it
How could they
Its custom made
My vocabulary won't participate in attempting to
explain to them
So, I just run to you
The one I don't need words with
But can talk to for hours
Searching for new ways to say
Thank you
Creativity prayed for from divine sources because only
God can help me explain
What hands have prayed for
What I was made for...
To love him
On purpose
Like I mean it
And I mean its
The best things I've ever felt...

to Webster

Hold up
Wait a minute
It's called my heart and guess who's up in it
Mr. Wortham
Double the "U"
To say he makes me happy is not close to the truth
Try elated
My heart overflowed
Like free Hennessey
For the cup on the road
So I ....
Take a moment to reflect
Give the utmost respect
And double his beck
With a call
You know what I mean
The kind you hear midst of hollas and screams
I mean excuse me
That's not lady like
It's just I've dreamt his company since I was a tike
And now my slumbers manifested
He kissed me and blessed it
No longer do I stress it
For he touched and caressed it
My soul
Never the same
Better than a friend
And there's no one to blame

But fate
For our paths have intertwined
Become one like our minds
And it's right
On
Time

new love/old love

I remember out nights turning into days as we sat and
talked about everything and nothing
When voicemails were filled with you singing your
hearts joy to me
But my memory of them is far too strong to settle for
my current situation
I've found myself wondering if compromising for the
sake of love is the same as just compromising yourself
The question is not do I love you
But do you love me with the same amount of passion
Someone told me love is a verb
A series of actions to let a person know you care
I remember when you loved me
I remember when I was afraid to love you
But willing to face that fear because you promised it
would be worth my while
It only hurts if you feel it
The pain I mean
The paid you said wouldn't come
I told you of my past experiences
And you said you would make it right
And at first you did
At first those late night calls filled with laughter cured
all my ailments
Those messages that left melodic chants in my head
throughout the day helped
But then you forgot your promise
And I forgot my worth

And allowed myself to love and not be loved in return
You are the one who continues to be the one
But that passion you once had seems lost
But my memory has found a chance
For us
To be
again

letting go

He was in love
But now he's not
Don't know what I did or how to stop
I used to be the one to make him hot
He was in love
But now he's not
He use to kiss me then he quit
He'd heat me up like a fiery pit
Now he's talking hella mmm..
He used to kiss me
Then he quit
He used to touch me with love and concern
His hands so holt my skin would burn
Now at nice we toss and turn
He used to touch with love and concern
We used to dance to the beat of our hearts
Didn't know how to stop only how to start
And now we spend out days apart
We used to dance to the beat of our hearts
He use to love me
Now he don't
He used to kiss m
Then he quit
He used to touch me
Now he don't
We're through

epiphany

He me had
Me had he
I was him
He was me
We were each other
But the rain it fell with fierce light and thunder
The love we once shared was placed asunder
No more *togetha*
Yet this tale I tell is not of pain or woe
For the attraction, we felt will forever grow
We still *lovin*
Though we caused more pain that most would take
Somehow, we share a bond no force could break
We are inseparable
And though we did more harm than sometimes good
I'd hold you this moment if only I could
I guess I'm *iggin*
But he showed me things no other man could show
And with him I grew more than I thought I'd grow
I am enlightened.

Don't let go yet

Like wombs
Occupied by premature hope
Hands in fists
Preparing for battles they don't exist
Stretch

As raindrops dance against windows of moving cars
We speed
We race
To chase identities moving quicker
Copies of a copy
Only faded pictures
Copies of a copy
Distorted depicters
Hands tights on the wheels
As thoughts get shook like Richter

We drive to be loose
We drive to be free
And we'll bust speakers so you know you *aint* as good
as me

But fingertips slip
Our grip we forget
 Next stops the top
 Don't let go yet

We claim change like dimes
Burnt offering we bring
Choosing sacrifices over repentance
Wondering which one He'll see
Trying to build stairways to heaven
Only nailing him to the tree
Bound in our afflictions when we've already been set
free

Release
Is what we want to say
As we are flooded by life
Headed for battle by the day
By the way
The world turns on its axis
We rotate our position
Trying to gain access
Like that woman with the issue
Be determined don't fret
Hold tight to his garment
Don't let go yet

Find my dream

I'm going to climb every mountain
I'm going to swim every stream
I'm going to follow every rainbow til I find my dream
Since May 27th, 1983 it seems
I've been destined for greatness
A piece of the American Dream
So, I flirted with the idea on April 11th it was conceived
And on May 14th 2012
J Parle' came to be
And the story's still being written
So, I'm believing BIG and praying BOLD
'Cause He'd never give me vision
If it wasn't mine to hold
Billionaire status
Reppin' my tribe
Building my team
I ain't trying to go to rehab
I love being a J Parle' fiend

Solomon

I dreamt of you last night
You were perfect
Like more perfect than I knew existed
A tapestry of love
Here in flesh
For me to touch
And kiss
And love
I dreamt of you
That mischievous grin like your father
Congenial
Straight forwardness like your mother
I have to teach you to tone down your passion even
though I don't want to
I dreamt of you last night Solomon
Yours eyes looked into mine like I was a god
Like you didn't have the power break me at your whim
Like I wasn't a slave to your happiness
I dreamt of you sunny
The ringlets in your hair
You hate them bc they aren't like the other boys
I love them and tell you to stand out
I can tell you only do it to make me happy but it makes
me smile
I dreamt of you
My little Appleseed
Waiting for you to come true
8/3/13

Jonah

You're like the best parts of both
How you manage to make early alright
Strong enough to handle it
I could kiss you all day
You my sweet baby
Fat cheeks
Fatter heart
Destined you are for greatness
Little brother
Big example of love
Smile as contagious as they come
Blessings
So, large
In such a tender frame
What have I done to deserve you
My dove
Sweet like your coos
Warm as Sister Racheal's hugs
Happy as promise
You are a dream come true

Cry

Sometimes you've got to cry
Life gets
Heavy
We get filled with so much....
Stuff
So much stuff we can't move
So much stuff we can't breathe
So much stuff we gotta cry
Let it out
Lighten loads
Get free
Sometimes
Eyes remember
What heads try to forget
They run away
Tears
Down faces of broke hearted
Down faces of the disappointed
Tears fall because they got too much stuff to carry
Try to balance what it means
Try to balance the thought of no other half
Tyr to balance optimism with fact
Fact?
Or fear
Choosing faith
Gaining relief
Sometimes we cry
Because we don't get it

All this stuff
Maybe I've used too much happiness
We get hungry for more
Can't wait
Frustration drowns us in tears
Sometimes we cry
To gain enough strength to move forward
Let tears fall to our shoulders
What's it mean?
Means we are strong enough to feel
Means we're real
Means we've got what it takes to handle all this...
Stuff

at the altar

I messed up again
Seems like no matter which way I turn I run smack dab
into sin
And I keep thinking
If I really loved you I wouldn't fall
If our relationship was really strong, I wouldn't disgrace
the name that's above all
Why do I keep yielding to sin?
Knowing the fruits of temptation are the devils only
friend
Knowing I want no covenant with him
I keep thinking his thoughts
And filling his cup to the brim
With lust and falsification
Sending my covenant with the Lord on temporary
vacation
Thinking how did I get caught up again
Knowing this time is the last time I bend
To this sin
Messed up again
Messed up again
I ran smack dab into sin
Forgive me

tick tock

Tickin' tickin' tickin' on my time clock to deliverance
Tick *ticktockin'* on my time clock to deliverance
Got to get this right
Got to get this right
on
Time
Seems to be against me, but I know it's my best friend
while I'm tick
Tick *ticktockin'* on my
Time clock to deliverance
To be delivered out of
That place I was in
That habit I was in
Looking for the Holy Spirit to guide me
And keep me
Tick *ticktickin'* on my time clock to deliverance
'Cause I've got to get away from where I am
Got to keep on tick *ticktickin'*
Tick *ticktockin'* on

I am a poem

I am poem created by God
For his name sake
I have been molded, thought about, meditated on
Every word line and stanza was created for me
I am His creation
Placed on this earth not by force, but by faith
And if the words get rearranged don't worry there will come
a change
A change in restoration
To fix up
To make right the wrong
In the name of Christ
I will splash the paper with his blood
And rearrange the words as they are saturated in the Anointing
I am a poem that you don't have to worry if you don't understand
For this poem was not created by man
It cannot be read by use of eye, ear, or mind
It's in a language only the spirit can find
And when the blindness ceases and the tongue confesses the
truth can my poem be absorbed from leaflet to root
I am a poem
Created by God
Formed in His word
Restored in His Love

1 Samuel 30:8

God said it's out there for me
So I search and know it will be found
No matter the raiding parties
Obstacles great or small
I will pursue and recover all

So a man thinketh, so he is
I have more than a conqueror in this holy sanctuary
So in no level of fear will I ever fall
I shall pursue and recover all

There are those in the midst not standing on the word
Settling not for first, sometimes second or third
Of God's best
Thinking I should too
But I know a way maker that will pull me through
So I don't care if I have to run, walk, or crawl
I will pursue and recover all

All
Not a few or some
For through worship I know this feat is already won
It is written we can do all things
So on that irrefutable fact shall I forever cling
This life is for the living
And I will have a ball
Because I will pursue
And recover

All

Propitiation

Sweetest thing I've ever known
Formed in the beginning when God from His throne
Created the heavens and the earth
And from the earth Adam and Eve
Breathed in them the breath of life
Even though from that life He knew He'd grieve
But grief begat mercy
And mercy begat life
And Life begat redemption from human sin and strife
For God so loved the world that He gave his only son
That whosoever would believe
Could live constantly with the one
Or the three
Father, son, and spirit
And when you meditate on the word you can't help but
feel it
When you think of His kindness and Agape sacrifice
I'd be sad to think of existence without the existence of
Christ
That came
So, we could have life
And have life more abundantly
Despite the sin disease that drew us to the tree
It was our sin disease that drew Him to the tree
The cross
To offer up His life that we may not be life
But when He came he said to love
To forgive and love some more

To believe and to receive
And to know down to your core that
Christ is the savior
Gods only son
Offered as endurance in this race we steady run
For we shall not be weary in this race we steady run and
run
And run
That eventually will be won
And as we cross the finish line with beads of
perspiration
As I offer from my beings these words of exhortation
As I thank God for the Christ and the spirit of
preparation
As I live my life in holy exclamation
That Jesus is the Christ
And in Him I will believe
For He hung
Bled
And died
And rose again for me
Because of who He is
Was
And will always be
I say with confidence
I
Have been
REDEEMED

In the Words of Isaiah

Young the age
Old the tears
Unnecessary my weary body
Lord, I know those that wait on you shall renew their
strength
So the question I'm left asking myself is, "What am I
waiting for?"
There were
And are
Too many times I thought I had the situation under
control
When I thought I could do this on my own
And every time I fell you picked me up
Dusted me off and sent me on my way
Never forcing your salvation
Just leaving it to me to accept the things that I could not
do for myself
So I accepted your love
Your mercy
And grace
While I continued to disgrace myself in your presence
So years
And tears later
I'm back
With a greater sense of understanding
For now I know you were just waiting on me
To wait on you
So that my strength could be renewed

So my tears could be dried
So that I could praise you
Wholly

lyrically speaking

Lyrically speaking
I can hold my own
I take a schismatic rhetoric
And create me a thrown
This life is my own
You can call me your highness
Try as you may
You still cant find this
Type of flow
See the words come from inside me
Often so bright that they often seem to blind me
But I continue the fight
Considering beauty my mind and mouth
Consummating their marriage at the mic
I wanna be free and that be ok
So on times like today
I can say
It aint always been honky dory
And in fact you'll understand you'll never get the full
story
There was guts to this glory
Yet you wonder how my words get formed
They're often the rainbow at the end of my storm
When I'm thinking
If I don't write this down
If I don't write this down
If I don't write this down right now I'll die

So why beg the question
I freely give answers
My people are plagued because they let their tongue be
their cancer
I see it eat away their hope
Trying to turn truths into fallacies in an effort to cope
With the issue at hand
Too many sistas trying to find God in a man
And can't understand
Why they cry every night
Losing love every second
Holding on too tight
To not so
And so they go
On this search to find themselves
Finding only a hoe
Only a foe
And still don't know why
If I don't write this down right now I'll die
And the moments get so intense
Heart beating faster every moment
Mouth muscles start to clinch
Or was that shake
I'm afraid of the impact my next words could make
So I get nauseas
Cause I'm all too cautious
Of what the outcome could be
But I firmly believe what's freedom if you ain't free
Ain't my cup of tea
So I face this fear

Lump in my throat as I try to hold back tears
That give too much fact
Cause when honestly meets the audience I don't know
how to act
Mouth muscles contract
Teeth grit
Trying to deal with this
Shit
As I'm climbing walls
And praying to day I don't fall from
The pressure
And if I don't write this down
If I don't write this down
If I don't write this down
Right now
I'll die
So why ask why
Some things are as they is
My first real passion to enter the biz
Not for the dough
All I ever wanted to do was rock just one show
Left brain versus right
But with all that's going on
I'm living to make these words right
Make this flow tight
Make sure you feel me
Cause with all things created equal I wonder what my
score would be
Again, left wondering exactly how free is free
And if I don't write this down

If I don't write this down
If I don't write this down right now
I'll die.

Beautiful and Strange

Beautiful
As the first time you believed in yourself
Strange
As every moment prior that you didn't
How did we miss this
Gift
How did we miss the power we held in our womb
We are creators
Feels like somethings brewing
I can't call it
Would if I could
Seems like somethings missing
Can't call it
I wouldn't if I could
Beautiful
As that time you accepted your lovers hand
Beautiful
As realizing it was you all along
Strange
As every time you doubted your potential
Who knew
Life could be
Like this
Who knew
All I had to do
Was be

Beautiful
As sunrises
As words of encouragement
As inspiration
Strange
As defining you for you
As not believing anything contrary
Strange as being the authority over your life
Beautiful as remembering
It's all a process
That forgiveness still works
Strange as second chances
As still loving
Strange as trusting intuition no one can comprehend
Beautiful as a heart that keeps reaching
Beautiful as a heart that keeps loving
Beautiful as every soul that keeps dreaming
Beautiful as every soul that keeps giving
Beautiful as every heartbroken person trying again
Beautiful as tenacity
Beautiful as integrity
Beautiful as using words to heal
Using words to build
Using words to soothe
Using faith to keep going
Strange as every moment prior that you didn't
How did we miss this
Gift
How did we miss the power we held in our womb
We are creators

Feels like somethings brewing
I can't call it
I would if I could
Somethings missing
Can't call it
I wouldn't if I could

About the Author

Jerica D. Wortham is a Tulsa, OK native with an international spirit. Jerica has been writing, and performing her poetry since the tender age of 11. In May 2012 Jerica founded J PARLE' LLC, and started J PARLE' Literary Magazine. This endeavor gathered artists from all around the country, and provided a platform to those that were in some instances more comfortable with the pen than the mic.... The mission: to give every voice a chance to be heard. In 2013 she was presented with the opportunity to host her very first live show; and J PARLE' Live was born! An author and philanthropist, in October 2014 she founded the J Parle' Scholarship fund where she was able to award local students and adults with money to continue or pursue their education. When she is not working, she enjoys spending time with her husband Webster, and their two sons Solomon and Jonah.

Made in the USA
Columbia, SC
29 February 2020